Great Minds Think Alike

11 Quotes to Inspire You to Ignite Your Passion and Find Your Purpose

"Every life has a purpose. We need to let go of the past. Live in the present. Do not waste today worrying about what will happen tomorrow. Embrace your true spirit, embrace and listen to grace and you will be transformed in the moment. Do not fixate on what you want but give thanks for what you have."

~ Caroline Myss ~

"I believe we're all put on this planet for a purpose, and we all have a different purpose."

~ Ellen DeGeneres ~

"There is no greater gift you can give or receive than to honor your calling. It's why you were born. And how you become most truly alive."

~ Oprah Winfrey ~

"Work with purpose is passion. Work without purpose is punishment."

~ Jillian Michaels ~

"Allow your passion to become your purpose, and it will one day become your profession."

~ Gabrielle Bernstein ~

"You can't connect the dots looking forward; you can only connect them looking backwards. So you have to trust that the dots will somehow connect in your future. You have to trust in something — your gut, destiny, life, karma, whatever. This approach has never let me down, and it has made all the difference in my life."

~ **Steve Jobs** ~

"The things you are passionate about are not random, they are your calling."

~ **Fabienne Fredrickson** ~

"Pay attention to the things you are naturally drawn to. They are often connected to your path, passion, and purpose in life. Have the courage to follow them."

~ **Ruben Chavez** ~

"When your passion and purpose are greater than your fears and excuses, you will find a way."

~ **Unknown** ~

"Purpose is the reason you journey. Passion is the fire that lights the way."

~ **Unknown** ~

"Your purpose in life is to use your gifts and talents to help other people. Your journey in life teaches you how to do that."

~ **Tom Krause** ~

Ignite Your
PASSION

Find Your
PURPOSE

IGNITE YOUR PASSION
FIND YOUR PURPOSE

Live Your Best Life at 50 & Beyond

Carol Ann DeSimine

Copyright © 2024 by Carol Ann DeSimine

All rights reserved.

Published in the United States by:

Carol Ann DeSimine, MPR
Goddess55 Publishing
Sewell, NJ 08080
www.Goddess55.com

Editing/Layout/Publishing: www.Goddess55.com
Cover Design: Carol Ann DeSimine
Author's Photographer: Richard L. Grupenhoff

This book is protected by copyright. No part of this book may be used or reproduced in any manner whatsoever; electronic or mechanical, including photography, recording, or by any information storage and retrieval system or technologies now known or later developed, without written permission of the author except in the case of brief quotations embodied in critical articles and reviews.

To contact the author, email carolanndes12@gmail.com.

Printed in the United States of America.

~ Dedication ~

This book is dedicated to my grandchildren,
Charly Grace Newlin and J.T. Newlin.
May you live a life of purpose where you are free to
express your gifts at your highest potential.

And to their parents, Jason Newlin and Cindy Decker, who are
wise enough to recognize those gifts and generous enough to
provide them with the opportunities that support them to
live into their potential.

~ Contents ~

Introduction: Your Path to Purpose Starts Here 11

Part I: Take the STAGES Assessment 19

    Chapter 1. The STAGES Life Purpose Formula 21

    Chapter 2. STAGE 1: Standards 27

    Chapter 3. STAGE 2: Talent 35

    Chapter 4. STAGE 3: Abilities 39

    Chapter 5. STAGE 4: Gifts 43

    Chapter 6. STAGE 5: Experience 49

    Chapter 7. STAGE 6: Story 57

Part II: The Next Stage: Live Your Purpose 71

    Chapter 8. Putting It All Together 73

    Chapter 9. What to Do With It? 79

    Chapter 10. Mindset 101: The Invisible Force 93

Epilogue 99

Acknowledgments 101

Resources 102

About the Author 103

INTRODUCTION
Your Path to Purpose Starts Here

> "If you can't figure out your purpose, figure out your passion. For your passion will lead you right into your purpose."
>
> ~ Bishop T.D. Jakes ~

passion — *a strong or extravagant fondness, enthusiasm, or desire for something.*

Welcome Goddess! I am so glad you found your way here. Because you're reading this book, I'm guessing you're searching for more passion and purpose in life. You might be at a crossroads, whether it's an inner voice calling you to be more and do more, or a life event that's causing you to make a change, and you see it as an opportunity to finally have life your way.

What does *your way* look like?

It's common for women, especially around age 50, to wake up one day and realize you've been going through the motions, living by someone else's rules, playing the good girl, good mother, and good wife. There's nothing wrong with that — it's quite satisfying and rewarding to be a mother raising amazing humans. But it's inevitable that our little darlings grow up and go off on their own, leaving a void to fill.

Even if that's not the case, many women get to a certain age and feel a tugging of their heart strings to be more, do more, and have more — whether it's material wealth, spiritual fulfillment, or a longing to make a bigger impact in the world.

Some women find their purpose early on and spend their life living on purpose, but that's very rare. Even if you've got the cushy job with the corner office overlooking the lake and a 6-figure salary, it's common to wake up one day, questioning, *Is this all there is?*

This is commonly called a *midlife crisis* but I see it as an awakening of who you truly are.

Life's Transition Points

Consider yourself lucky if your worst-case scenario is that you've outgrown your current situation and are in a position to take control of your future. If you're in a position where you're forced to make a change, there is a tendency to settle for less than you deserve. There's still the question, however, of, *What do I do next?* Age 50 is too young to retire, but it's old enough to feel the crunch of time passing and wonder if there's enough left to start a new venture. If you find yourself in any of the common situations below, you might rush into your next chapter out of survival, without taking time to pause and reflect on the deeper meaning of the event.

Do any of these describe your current situation...

> ➤ Were you downsized from a job with no other prospects in sight?

> ➤ Are you suddenly single, left to fend for yourself?

> ➤ Are you're healing from the loss of a loved one, and can't bring yourself to go back to what life used to be?

> ➤ Do changes in the workplace leave you feeling obsolete and insignificant?

- Are you the caretaker of a family member, stressed and stretched as you try to balance additional responsibilities with a 9 to 5 job?
- Have office politics made the workplace unbearable to the point where you don't fit in any longer?
- Are you part of the Great Resignation and still searching for that freedom-based lifestyle you were promised?

If you see yourself in any of these situations, know that you are not alone. Events like these are more common than you realize, and they're seldom planned for. They are transition points that force you to change your life. You can choose to replace one bad situation with another, or you can see this as your opportunity to spread your wings like the beautiful butterfly that you are and pursue your passion to live a life of greater purpose. But this begs the question: *How do you know what your true purpose is?*

Passion v. Purpose

We often confuse *passion* with *purpose*, but there is a clear distinction. *Passion* is the enthusiasm or desire you feel toward something. It's what excites you, what brings you joy, and what you love to do. Passions can be diverse, ranging from hobbies such as painting or gardening to interests such as cooking or traveling. Your passions are what make you feel alive and engaged with life. Passions change and evolve over time, according to shifting interests and experiences.

Purpose, on the other hand, goes beyond mere enjoyment or excitement. It's the deeper reason behind what you do — the underlying meaning or significance that gives your life direction and fulfillment. Your purpose is about how you contribute to the world, how you make a difference and impact others. It's the sense of satisfaction that comes from aligning your actions with your values and beliefs, and using strengths and talents to serve something greater than yourself.

How to use this book

This book is designed to help you sift through your many passions to identify your purpose — what you are uniquely designed to do.

In Part I, I take you through my STAGES Life Purpose Formula, the process I used when I was at a crossroad in my business and had fallen out of alignment with the work I'd been doing for years.

Through soul searching, reflecting and evaluating, the STAGES process revealed my gifts, desires, life experiences, and what I was uniquely qualified to do. It was laid out before me, and I realized it all fell into a perfectly designed pattern that led to my finding my purpose. I started using the process with my clients and it was like magic: It revealed their purpose, the real problem they solve for their clients, and who their ideal clients are!

There is plenty of space to journal in the spaces provided, so all of your insights will be contained within the pages of this book.

In Part II, I provide some direction and ways to get your purpose out into the world, as well as some resources to help you. This is your time to unleash your Inner Goddess and play full out and fully expressed — without having to build like you did when you were 30, so everything I suggest is what I feel is path of least resistance.

Speaking of resistance, it's what I call "the silent killer of dreams," and it's all about mindset. So, I end each chapter with three mindset shifts. These help to summarize the main points of each chapter and highlight where you may need to shift your way of thinking.

Finally, I share parts of my life in short stories to share the humanness of a typical path to purpose. I've had many turning points, as you will see. My story is not written chronologically, but in snippets that relate to each chapter. This serves two purposes:

(1) Illustrating real-life experiences will help to you understand the content at the heart level..

(2) My story provides glimpses into a journey that may be similar to yours, with common threads that are universal to many women, especially those over age 50.

My hope is that the STAGES Life Purpose Formula, along with the stories and resources, will help ignite your passions and within them find your deeper purpose — to lead you to greater joy and fulfillment in your work and in life, as it did for me.

I also hope it helps you to see greater possibilities for yourself. Most of us have been taught to believe that life is short, but when you reach 50 you start to see that life is long.

When you focus forward, you realize you have many years ahead of you; when you reflect on the past, you see how everything you've done up to now has prepared you for this moment.

My wish is that STAGES ignites the courage within you to step into your next chapter with confidence and inspires you to reach for your biggest dreams!

With love,

Carol Ann

> **Most of us have been taught to believe that life is short, but when you reach 50 you start to see that life is long."**

~ Mindset Shifts ~

For each chapter I'll give you three points to ponder. These serve as a recap of the main takeaways for each chapter and give you cause for reflection. You may even want to journal on them so they really sink in. Your first mindset shift is in regards to the Introduction of this book and what to keep in mind as you move forward.

> A *midlife crisis* is your soul's awakening to who you truly are. It commonly happens around age 50 because that's a natural turning point that makes you question: *Is this all there is?* Kids are fleeing the nest around this age, too, which leaves a void to fill. You're also in a different place of opportunity, where you can choose to stop building and start leading with your wisdom and experience

> Passion often leads to purpose. If you're at a crossroad, it's common to want to take the safe path and transition to another J.O.B. just to survive, but it's a great opportunity to step into your higher potential and thrive.

> Passion brings joy to life, but a purpose gives life meaning. A passion may provide hours of enjoyment to you, but your purpose is about having an impact on the lives of others and making your mark in the world!

Now, let's get you started on your path to igniting your passions so that you find your purpose, but first I'll provide some context on what led me to write this book in the first place!

~ My Story, Part 1 ~
The Sudden Exodus

At my work desk, Glassboro, NJ, c. 1990.

I changed my life at age 50. I thought I was content in my job of 18 years, working for an educational organization that specialized in creative problem solving for students. But when I got blamed for some small thing that I absolutely did not do, I walked out.

Even though I was applying many of my passions in that job, discontent had been setting in for a while. It took only one comment that day to put me over the edge to say, "I've had enough." It was a rash move, but deep down, I knew there had to be more for me. I had honed many skills and talents in that job, some I could call *passions*. But my passions became so routine that they lost their meaning.

I had hit a glass ceiling with no room for growth. I was helping someone else achieve their dream while putting mine on the back burner. I was so caught up in working for someone else that I wasn't even conscious of any bigger dreams of my own.

But I must have had them, because, on reflection, I realize there had been a soft whisper in my ear, calling me to express my greater potential and step into my higher purpose. I ignored it, until I couldn't any longer. That one wrong comment was the impetus that compelled me to answer that calling and change the entire trajectory of my life.

Here I was, 50 years old, at a crossroad with no plan of what to do next. But I was excited. Somehow, I knew life would work out for me. It did, until it didn't. And then it did again

Ignite Your Passion • Find Your Purpose

PART I

The STAGES Life Purpose Formula

Chapter 1

The STAGES Life Purpose Formula ~
The Key to Finding Your Higher Purpose

"Your life will never lie to you; it is always seeking your own good. Accessing the power of your own purpose is the practice of listening in to what your life is saying to you."
~ Mary Morrissey ~

stage — *a step or degree in a process; a particular phase or period of development.*

I don't recommend you do something as rash as I did and walk out of a job that's helping to pay your bills, but I do recommend that if you're at a crossroad, whether it's your inner voice calling or an upset caused by a life event, you see it as an opportunity to pursue the passion that leads to your purpose and start taking the steps to live it *now*. That's what we're going to do with the STAGES Life Purpose Formula.

What is STAGES and how can it help you?

STAGES is a 6-step process designed to help you identify your purpose. You might think of this as your life purpose, or your soul's calling. I think of these as one and the same. We are always living our purpose — what we need to be doing or being at different times in our life, for different people, and in different circumstances. But it's always evolving and leading us to our higher purpose. Some call this your *soul's destiny*. Everything that's happened up to now is preparation for what's to come. And just when you get comfortable in one evolution of your purpose, that whispering voice will again start to call you to be more and do more.

Whatever you're going through now, whether you perceive it as good or bad, know that every breakdown is the impetus for a breakthrough that adds another element of meaning to your life and directs you on your path as you pursue your destiny.

For the purpose of this book, our intention is to find the passion that is your purpose *now*, knowing that it will evolve over time. Stay open to possibility and don't feel that you have to be 100 percent certain that whatever you choose is what you'll be stuck with for life. You get to change if and when you want. Going through STAGES will help reveal the ONE path that is most likely to bring you success *now*. All it takes is one baby step to get started in the direction of your purpose, so consider reading this book that first step.

Take the Assessment

The STAGES Life Purpose Formula is not another personality test or career quiz — it's a comprehensive framework that takes you on an inner exploration to find out who you are at the soul level. By guiding you through a series of thought-provoking questions and exercises you'll gain clarity on what truly matters to you and what you're uniquely positioned to offer the world. STAGES is an acronym for the six areas that you'll assess:

- ➤ **Standards** determine what's most important to you in life. By identifying your top core values, likes and dislikes, and your big WHY you'll clarify what truly matters to you and what brings you joy. You'll gain valuable insights into your authentic self and the desires that bring fulfillment.

➤ **Talents** are the innate passions you've cultivated that come natural to you and that others recognize in you. By embracing your unique talents, you'll gain clarity on how they can be used to make a meaningful impact in the world.

➤ **Abilities** are tasks and skills that you've acquired over the years. These are strengths and core competencies that can contribute to your success in whatever endeavor you choose.

➤ **Gifts** are your superpowers, the special qualities or attributes that you may have hidden or played down because they are so unique and often misunderstood. By honoring your gifts, you gain a deeper appreciation for what sets you apart from others.

➤ **Experience** is what you've earned and learned — your credentials as well as the life lessons that shaped your journey. Reflecting on the insights and wisdom gained through past experiences will uncover themes, patterns, and opportunities that have led you toward your purpose.

➤ **Story** is the narrative of the life experiences that shaped your purpose. Within your story lies the meaningful message you can share with others to inspire, motivate, teach, and heal.

As you explore each stage, you'll gain clarity, confidence, and direction in discovering your life purpose and creating a life of fulfillment. You'll uncover the unique combination of contributions you have to offer the world and the potential that awaits you. With this newfound clarity as your compass, you'll be empowered to reignite your passions, embrace those that reveal your purpose, and apply them to helping others, while helping you live your best life.

In the following chapters, you'll assess each STAGE to the best of your ability. This is about you, and it's up to your own interpretation, so there's no right or wrong way to do any of it.

This is also an exercise in tapping into your inner knowing and trusting your intuition. As you go through each STAGE, write down your first responses, then go back and read what you wrote. Sleep on it. Journal on the prompts. You'll want to tweak your responses, and that's a good thing. You'll find that there's overlap and that's okay.

Expect to be pleasantly surprised. You will have immediate insights, and some areas will require deeper contemplation. You will remember things from your past that were long forgotten — the bad and the good. Try not to dwell on the negative. This is meant to be fun and to learn about who you are, so shine brightly as you sort through every aspect of your life.

After going through all six stages, you'll notice the "golden thread" that runs through your life experiences, as if you're spinning a tapestry that is finally coming together. That is your TRUTH, and the biggest clue to finding your purpose.

It's important to remember, though, as you journey through the STAGES of your life, that your purpose is not a destination to reach someday — it's a path to walk every day with courage and grace, propelled by your passions. Hold this intention as you embrace the beauty of self-exploration. Step into the fullness of who you are now, knowing that you're evolving into who you are meant to be, and that the best is yet to come.

Are you ready? Take a few deep breaths and let's start exploring the inner you!

> **" you'll notice the 'golden thread' that runs through your life experiences, as if you're spinning a tapestry that is finally coming together."**

~ Mindset Shifts ~

➤ You are living your purpose now, but it's always evolving and leading you to your higher purpose. This is your soul's destiny. The intention of STAGES is to help you find the passion that is your purpose now, with the understanding that it will evolve over time.

➤ STAGES Life Purpose Formula is not another personality test or career quiz—it's a series of thought-provoking questions and exercises to help you gain clarity on what truly matters to you and what you're uniquely positioned to offer the world.

➤ After going through all six stages, you'll notice the "golden thread" that runs through your life. That is the biggest clue to finding your purpose.

~ My Story, Part 2 ~
The Best Decision I Could Have Made

After I left my J.O.B., I was burned out so I gave myself 6 months to figure out what my next stage of life would be for me.

I went on a few job interviews with non-profit organizations. None paid that well, and at each interview I heard a version of "You're overqualified." One woman told me I wouldn't be happy there. Another told me there would be "nowhere for me to go." I admired those women and would have accepted positions simply to learn from them, but they saw something in me that I couldn't see for myself.

Here I was, wondering if I was good enough to be offered a position and, turns out, they were trying to tell me that I was too good! The deal-breaker was that none offered the kind of vacation package I was used to.

I had no desire to start my own business, but I had to do something. So, exactly 6 months from the day I walked out of my job, I sat at my computer desk and said to myself, out loud:

"Carol Ann, you're going to try this entrepreneurship thing, but if you don't replace the salary you made in that full-time job, you're going to have to go find another one."

I marched down to the County office and registered my company name, Big Eye Media, Photography and Design — a creative services agency. I joined a few networking events, told my colleagues I was open for business, and I was on my way.

Turns out I made the right decision. I went on to earn 6 figures my very first year, nearly double what I was being paid as an employee.

Was starting a business fulfilling my purpose? At that time, yes. My quick success was confirmation that it was the right thing to do; it built my confidence and served as a stepping stone for what was to come.

Circa 2010, Turnersville, New Jersey. Joining networking groups connected me with the local community where I forged many friendships. Here I am with Laini Bianculli (l.) and Denise DiPaoli (center). A press release I wrote and distributed for Laini got her on the cover of MD Magazine as their beauty expert. At that time, you could find it in just about every doctor's office in the U.S. so she was thrilled at the exposure!

Chapter 2

STAGE 1: Standards
What is most important to you?

"When you're clear, what you want will show up in your life and only to the extent that you're clear."
~ Janet Atwood ~

standard – *a basis of measure, value, comparison, or judgment.*

The first STAGE of finding the passion that leads to your purpose is to identify what you need in your life to be happy, or at least satisfied, by examining these three areas: *core values, likes and dislikes,* and the *WHY* that drives your bigger vision.

We all operate from a set of individual standards, both consciously and unconsciously. We know what we like; we know what we don't like. We know what's essential for us to be happy and what we won't tolerate.

Identifying your standards serves as the measure to do more of what you love, and to stop tolerating what doesn't serve you. The key is to be clear on what you want your life to be and what you require to be truly happy. The first standard we'll explore are the values you live your life by, commonly known as *core values*.

Standard 1. Identify Your Core Values

Core values can be defined as "fundamental beliefs and principles that guide our behavior and decision-making." They represent qualities that are most important to us in life and define what we stand for. Core values often serve as a compass that provides the inner guidance that steers the direction of our choices.

We all have many values that make up the essence of who we are: what it takes for us to be happy, how we view acceptable behavior, our priorities. They are a moral code, of sorts, that define right from wrong, in your opinion. Our core values determine how we react and operate in various situations, and they change in order of importance at different times in our life.

For example, *family* is a top core value for just about everyone. But, should it be at this stage of life? If you have young children that you provide for, the answer is probably an emphatic *yes*. But, if your kids are grown, and you're not responsible for their well-being any longer, *family* may move down a few notches on the values scale.

This does not mean family is less important to you, it's just that family doesn't require your attention so much, and that value frees up space for a value that is more pertinent to your own self-fulfillment.

Another common value that fluctuates in order of priority at different stages of life is *health*. In your 30's this may mean 6-pack abs and a hot body because you want to attract a mate. It's a value because you devote time, effort, and money to it, but are you valuing it for the right reasons or to meet someone else's standards? It's important, but not as crucial as it would be for someone in her 60's with arthritis that's limiting her activity, or someone with a life-threatening illness.

You'll find that you have core values for different areas of life, and you'll discern those here, too.

Before you move on, take a few minutes to quiet your mind and really focus on what's most important to you NOW.

What to Do

A. In the space below, brain dump 10-30 core values that are important to you. These are usually a one-word noun. There are hundreds of values to choose from, and brain-dumping is going to ignite your imagination and expand your thinking. You'll get more granular later but, for now, go broad. Some examples of values are *abundance, acceptance, empowerment, kindness, education, mastery, humor, zest, adventure, fun…*

B. Now let's get more specific by separating your values into categories. I believe we have a set of values that are important to us in our personal life, and another set for our professional life. We also have a bigger vision that might be based on lofty values that may seem far out of reach but align with your big dreams and desires. Determine which areas of life your values fit into. From your "A" list, choose 3 top core values for each of the categories below:

~ **LIFE VALUES:** These are the values that you need in your life and environment to be happy, healthy, and whole; for example, *spirituality, health, wellness, love, abundance, beauty, comfort, family, peace, joy...*

_____

_____

_____

~ **WORK VALUES:** These reflect what's important to you in your work life, and they also represent how you show up in your profession. You may dream of having your own business because you value *freedom* or, if you have a strong desire to help people, *service* might be a top value. For some, *creativity* is important to the work they do. Others might long for *respect* or *recognition*. Other examples of work values are *fun, quality, simplicity, alignment, commitment, ambition, decisiveness, accomplishment, advancement, zest, passion, purpose, leadership...*

_____

_____

_____

~ **VISION-RELATED VALUES:** While life values are more survival and needs based, and work values are fulfillment based, vision-related values are based on your aspirations. This is what you dream about and what you're working toward. For example, if you desire to become a published author, it's not really the book that you want, you might want recognition or to make an impact. These values are future-focused and outcome-based. A few more examples are *wealth, fame, leadership, stature, belonging, influence, support, fulfillment, ease...*

_____

_____

_____

You might need to move these around a few times as you determine what's truly important in each category. It can be difficult to narrow them down, but the more you do, the clearer you'll become.

Standard 2. Likes and Dislikes

While *core values* are defined by exploring the inner you, *likes and dislikes* are determined by the activities you do, and what you spend your time and money on. *Likes* could be passions or pastimes, such as knitting, cooking, or traveling. *Dislikes* are things you would not want to do or what you won't tolerate. For example, you might dislike exercising or attending networking events, or having to create Excel spreadsheets because they stifle your creativity.

A. Brainstorm up to 10 activities that you love to do. Then circle the top 3 that you could easily do all day, five days a week in a business where you get paid to do them.

_____

_____

_____

_____

_____

B. Now, list what you would NOT want to be doing on a regular basis. Be specific and realistic. You might not like selling, but that's part of business. Perhaps it's asking people for money that you really dislike. If you like to teach but don't like speaking to groups, you might not want to run live programs and, instead, offer digital courses.

_____
_____
_____
_____
_____

C. Write your top 3 likes and your top 3 dislikes here:

_____
_____
_____

Standard 3. What is Your BIG WHY?

Your WHY can be related to your core values and what you like to do, but it usually goes deeper. Your WHY is the reason behind whatever it is you choose to do. However, it does not have to be profound, or noble, or world changing. Your WHY is about YOU so don't worry about being viewed as selfish or self-serving. This is about YOUR self-actualization. It's perfectly fine if your WHY is to make a lot of money, get out of debt, feel fulfilled, have more freedom, become an influencer or media sensation, leave a legacy for your family, or to be able to get out of a job you hate. There's no right or wrong in any of this — think BIG!

Complete this statement: *My big WHY is to....*

_____
_____
_____
_____

~ Mindset Shifts ~

- Think of these as your **Selfish Standards.** Identifying your standards provides a measure of self-awareness and clarity of what you want your life to be and what you require to be truly happy.

- Core values are important because they define what's important to you in different areas of life. *Family* might be a life value, and *leadership* a work value, but the two may overlap so it's important to discern the difference. Vision-related values are what you are working toward and are usually more lofty than the values we're living now. These are our desires and greater potential.

- It's okay for your WHY to involve making a lot of money. You are not a charity case. When you align with your purpose to serve others, expect them to pay you. Serve yourself first, because unless you do, you won't be able to serve others effectively. If your top personal value is *family*, then a business value of *wealth* makes perfect sense, because in the end, it's all about supporting your family the best that you can, isn't it?

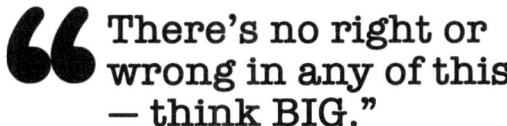

"There's no right or wrong in any of this — think BIG."

~ My Story, Part 3 ~
A Perfect Match of Values

In the 18 years I spent in that J.O.B., I got to further develop the skills that came naturally to me. Many people talk about manifesting their ideal job, but I believe that job manifested me. It was an educational organization that provided creative problem-solving activities for students of all ages. Family owned, and developed by a college professor, from my point of view, the values were *family, creativity*, and *fun*.

Onsite at a company event at Iowa State University, where I ran the press room and produced highlight videos. Circa 2003.

It was a match for my values, too. I was in the creative side of the business, and when the powers that be recognized my proclivity to certain tasks, they gave me more of that to do. I published books, wrote curriculum, served as the assistant editor of their newsletter. I became the in-house Quark Expert and got to do all the page layout and design. I worked with an editor from Columbia University on larger curriculum projects. It was a good learning experience.

I had quite a bit of freedom, as well as flexibility. My friends worked in the other department of the company, so I had friendships, too. We would go walking on our lunch hour. The owners treated us well. Several times a year they would take us to 5-star restaurants, hold parties, and we were like one big happy family. But then came the breakdown: a lawsuit that ultimately tore apart the friendships and family-like atmosphere. That was the end of one set of values that evolved into a different set.

It was a learning experience of life, but it's in events like these that the greatest growth occurs.

Chapter 3

STAGE 2: Talents
What comes natural to you that you've cultivated?

"Talent is nothing without persistence."
~ **Dean Crawford** ~

talent — *a special natural ability or aptitude.*

A talent is much more than what you're naturally good at. It's what you know you're good at, are driven to get better at, and devote a good amount of time and effort to.

Talents are abilities that you cultivate through application, practicing or studying — and then doing. A talent comes natural to you and is something you have a strong interest in pursuing. Talents are often associated with creative arts such as painting, writing, photography, graphic design, but they can also be things such as sports, public speaking, or academics.

Talents are often passions, too. I observe the talents of my close friends, whether it's cooking or knitting and crocheting beautiful pieces that are unique and stunning. Would they want to turn their talents into a business? Probably not at this stage of life. Some talents are best left as hobbies to enjoy.

It's time to assess your talents. Journal on the questions below, without holding back.

- What do you consider your natural talents?

_____
_____
_____

- What do people compliment you on most often?

_____
_____
_____

- What pastimes or hobbies are you naturally drawn to?

_____
_____
_____

Now, write down your top 1-5 talents. Circle those you could see yourself turning into a business.

_____
_____
_____

Of these talents, is there one that you could turn into an "identity" and make a profession out of? If so, use it in an "I AM" statement. For example, *I am a writer. I am a singer. I am a musician. I am a painter. I am a gourmet chef. I AM the designer of beautiful sweaters.* You get the idea!

I AM a _____

_____
_____

~ Mindset Shifts ~

▸ These are your **True Talents**, what comes natural to you. Because you've put in the time and effort to cultivate them, you deserve to be compensated for them if you decide to incorporate them into a business.

▸ Your talents are what make you special. They're not the only thing, as you'll see as we go along, but don't assume that everyone else is good at what you're good at. We usually play down our talents as "nothing special" because they come so easy to us.

▸ It's never too late to apply your talents. Grandma Moses started painting in earnest at age 78, although she had many passions early on. Martha Stewart modeled for the cover of the *Sports Illustrated* swimsuit issue at age 80. In every movie and every Broadway play, there are older adults filling important roles. Why not you?

~ My Story, Part 4 ~
When Talent Turns Into a J.O.B.

I guess you could say I had a lot of untapped talent that was revealed through my work in that J.O.B. Growing up, I didn't have a lot of creative influences other than my father. Dad sparked my creativity by teaching me to paint, to type, to play guitar, and to use my mind in different ways. When I was around 5 years old, he told me to "color outside of the lines." Talk about confusion! When my teachers were stressing neatness, he was telling me to be messy. Too bad I did not understand what he was saying at that time. As I came of age in the 1970's, I was not lured into the corporate mindset, or motivated by money. I was a free spirit, a hippie some might say who wanted to "do her thing."

While I learned a lot and honed many innate talents at that job, I also pursued many personal interests. I went back to school and earned a B.A. in Communications and an M.A. in Public Relations.

With Mom & Dad at an opening reception for my photography exhibit, circa 2001.

I became a fine art photographer, exhibiting my work in galleries in the Philadelphia area. I won awards and was invited to teach photography and photojournalism as an adjunct professor at the university where I earned my degrees.

Once I started my business, clients were asking me for professional portraits, which required a studio. So, I built a photography studio in our home. Local families wanted portraits in front of the fountains in our lake. Business owners and authors hired me for head shots. I became a photographic retouch artist, obliging women who wanted chins lifted and inches shaved from their waists. It was tedious work.

One of my greatest talents — what was once a driving passion — now felt like an obligation. This is a perfect example of how turning a talent into a business takes the joy out of it. In September 2017, after photographing the local Italian Festival, I put my camera down and haven't touched it since.

Was photography my purpose? Yes, at the time, but not in the way you might think. Upon reflection, I was grateful that I was able to bring people together to expose them to the arts. My exhibit openings were festive events with friends, families and colleagues attending. I often wonder about some: Would they be exposed to the arts if it were not for that, and what influence did I have in inspiring them to create and enjoy other forms of art?

Chapter 4

STAGE 3: Abilities
What skills are your strengths?

"Do the thing you're good at. Not many people are lucky enough to be so good at something."
~ **John Green,** *The Fault in Our Stars* ~

ability — *competence in an activity or occupation because of one's skill, training, or other qualification.*

By now, you've determined what's most important to you and you've identified the natural talents that you've cultivated. For STAGE 3 we're turning the focus on your more objective strengths: tasks and skills that you're highly capable of doing. We label these *abilities*. An *ability* is a skill that you can apply to get a job done, and it can also be a strength if you're exceptional at it, but it isn't necessarily a passion. You may not want to make a career out of an ability, but it can be useful in supporting your business or whatever endeavor you embark on.

Housework is a good example: You might be capable of cleaning your house until it shines, and it brings you joy to see it shine, but you wouldn't want to clean other people's homes for a living.

Or gardening. You may have a knack for it and it might even be a passion, but you wouldn't want to make it your day job.

Even something like yoga. You don't have to be great at yoga to teach it, and many studios will require you to be certified. Yoga is a passion for many, but is it a purpose?

For this STAGE, you're going to do a brain dump of your abilities. Stay focused on the tasks, skills, and strengths that would support you to live your purpose. Look at abilities from both sides — what you prefer to *not* do as well as what you don't mind doing.

Identifying your abilities will help you to gain confidence in your capacity to overcome challenges and achieve goals, and they will also support your success. When you have a business, there will always be tasks you'll have to do that you might not like doing, such as *bookkeeping, accounting, marketing, sales*. If you spent your career doing any of these things, they'll come in handy. And, if you don't like doing them, you could hire them out, eventually.

A. List your abilities here:

_____
_____
_____
_____
_____
_____
_____
_____
_____
_____
_____
_____
_____

B. Next, go through your list and cross out the abilities that you would not want to incorporate into your business, and circle the ones that you feel will be useful to you in business.

You should have an overview of what you are highly capable of doing, and you may even recognize a theme or pattern. Do you see a trend that leans toward a type of business that would make good use of your abilities? These could be the nuts-and-bolts tasks of running a business, or they could be at the center of your business.

~ Mindset Shifts ~

➤ These are your **Amazing Abilities**. Of course, you'll have too many abilities to list here, so choose the ones that you're really good at that will come in handy in the years to come.

➤ Like talents, there are abilities that will come natural to you. Think about what you *really* did in your career. Were you recognized for certain abilities and given certain tasks to do? Often, we're hired for one thing and then our position turns into something else when others recognize our strengths.

➤ Whatever your next chapter ends up being, your abilities will come in handy. Every business requires foundational tasks to be successful — sales, marketing, copywriting, technical skills, and being able to handle finances. Eventually, you'll be able to delegate what you don't want to do, but you need to have an understanding of how your business operates so you can delegate effectively. Things like messaging, pricing, and developing relationships have to come from you first.

> **❝ Identifying your abilities will help you to gain confidence in your capacity to overcome challenges and achieve goals."**

~ My Story, Part 5 ~
The One-Woman Show

After being told I was overqualified at every job interview I went on, I finally saw that I did not recognize my talent and skill as anything unusual. But when I looked around, I didn't see many people who could do what I was capable of doing. There were graphic designers, but they did not write copy. Photographers I knew were not designers, or publishers, or writers. In my J.O.B., I stepped up to the plate anytime something needed to be done. I was the public relations person, writing press releases, designing press kits, running the press room and dealing with media at an annual event that drew 40,000 attendees from around the globe. I became the video producer, the photographer, the graphic designer. I wrote curriculum and published books.

In 2012, I started working with a mentor Dr. Venus Opal Reese, who taught me to value my creativity and to heal my heart.

I don't write this to brag. I enjoyed everything I got to do, but I learned a huge lesson: value your skills, abilities and talents. Don't think that because something comes easy to you that it comes easy to everyone.

The more I did, the more I was given to do. I rose to the occasion, and in retrospect saw that I was underpaid and undervalued. But, those abilities paid off once I became an entrepreneur, because I also came away with some savvy business skills that led to my success. Later, when I worked with a mentor she would tell me over and over: "You are worth so much more than you were ever taught to believe."

Too bad I had to wait until I was in my mid-fifties to hear it.

Chapter 5

STAGE 4: Gifts
What is your superpower?

"The meaning of life is to find your gift.
The purpose of life is to give it away."

~ Pablo Picasso ~

gift — *a special ability or capacity; natural endowment.*

Contrary to what Picasso suggests, I do not believe you should give your gift away. I believe your gifts were given to you from God, Source, the Universe (substitute with whichever term/belief you prefer) to support you to live the lifestyle you deserve. But I do agree with Picasso that the meaning of life is to find your gift. That's what we're doing in STAGE 4, identifying the gifts that will help you to live a life of purpose.

There's a fine line between a *gift*, a *talent*, and an *ability*. A *gift* is an extraordinary talent or ability that comes natural to you; something that you don't have to hone or cultivate. It's just there. It's your superpower. For some, it might be a sixth sense.

Gifts differ from talents because you may not express them outwardly; they're part of who you are and what you do. As with a talent, you might cultivate your gift. Many creatives are considered gifted when their talent becomes extraordinary, such as the songwriter Carole King, for example.

Or, your gift might be intellectual, such as Matt Damon's character in *Good Will Hunting*. True genius is a gift, because it goes beyond what even the above average mind is capable of. Will Hunting chose to work as a janitor at MIT, in an environment where his gifts would be noticed and appreciated by his mentors. He was an anomaly.

There are physical gifts, as with David Beckham, the soccer superstar, and his ability to "bend" the ball into the net, as if it's controlled by a higher power. Or the many gymnasts who are able to achieve super-human feats with their bodies. These go beyond just talent.

There are spiritual gifts — the highly intuitive, the hands-on healers or psychics, and those who channel ascended masters or communicate with angels. We all possess a sixth sense of intuition that we can develop, but spiritual giftedness goes beyond inner knowing. It's the healer, the medical intuitive, the psychic medium who is extraordinary at communicating with invisible forces. Many of these gifts are hidden from the mainstream or played down because of skepticism, but they're now much more acceptable — and common.

Whatever comes natural to you that most people don't have or would find almost impossible to cultivate, that goes beyond the ordinary, can be considered a gift.

Your gift makes you a category of one. But is your gift your passion? And is it something you can do as a business in service of others?

Really think about this one. Gifts are given to us for a reason. I believe they are your true soul's calling, and it's your responsibility to honor them and use them.

If you need a prompt to identify your gifts, answer these questions:

What do you feel is your superpower?

_____
_____
_____
_____

What comes so easy to you, yet you are almost embarrassed to talk about it because it's beyond what most others are capable of?

_____
_____
_____
_____

List your gifts here, then circle the one that is most extraordinary that you could use for the benefit of others. Place a star next to any others that relate to that one.

_____
_____
_____
_____
_____
_____
_____
_____

I hope you know by now that your gifts really are special. In the next STAGE, we're going broader, with a bird's eye view of the influences over your entire lifetime.

~ Mindset Shifts ~

➤ These are your **Goddess Gifts** because they are so special and often spiritual in nature. They come natural to you, and only you. They were given to you by God, the Universe, Source, Allah, whomever you choose to attribute them to (if anyone or anything) and it is your responsibility to use them.

➤ Goddess Gifts hinge on the supernatural. If you've ever watched David Beckham kick a soccer ball from mid-field and see it curve before going directly into the net, it's almost as if a supernatural force is guiding it. This goes far beyond skill. Or, take hands-on healing. A doctor spends years studying how to heal disease according to the book; a gifted healer performs miracles by directing energy according to her inner knowing.

➤ It's your responsibility to use your gifts. Because they hinge on the supernatural, many people will hide their spiritual gifts, or play them down. I've heard many adults talk about how they saw angels as a child, or "monsters," and their parents attributed it to an overactive imagination and told them to stop, so they did, thinking it was wrong. They shut down their powers, only to reactivate them when they got older. Think about the movie *The Sixth Sense*. "I see dead people" is more common than you might think. What you choose to do with your special ability is up to you, but you don't have to hide it, and you don't have to give it away either!

❝ **Your gift makes you a category of one.**❞

~ My Story, Part 6 ~
My Gifts

Growing up, I felt different, but no one was talking about creativity back then. Luckily, my father encouraged it in me and my brothers. I was around age 10 when Dad taught me to play guitar. We would practice in his room after dinner, playing duets. I was pretty good for my age. I liked it, until he started teaching me chords and my little fingers found them too difficult to master. I had to work at it, so when warm weather came, and I heard the kids playing outside, that's where I preferred to be, and I soon lost interest in guitar.

Nature or nurture? Me and my 5 brothers, all gifted in our own way, even though we were raised by the same parents in the same environment. c. 1964.

My brother Chris, on the other hand, had a gift for guitar. One day, when Dad wanted to take the boys fishing, Chris resisted. So, Dad bribed him to go by promising to teach him to play *Let It Be* on guitar. Dad kept his promise, and Chris never stopped playing. He even wrote an original song to perform for his 3rd-grade class on the keyboard Mom bought him for Christmas. Later, he played in local bands. Many of my friends referred to him as "the next Jimi Hendrix." People still remember him for his guitar playing. He was also a gifted painter, writer and poet. In his high school senior year, he was voted "most creative."

My brother, Richard, only a year younger than Chris, skipped 3rd grade in school because he was so far beyond the other kids in his aptitude, especially in math. He went on to become highly successful through a passion project that combined Mom's love for crossword puzzles and Dad's love for computers. A computer programmer by trade, Richard was recognized for his intelligence and his ability. My guess is that he has a supernatural ability to see patterns that most of us don't see, and an understanding of technology that most don't have. Two brothers, same environment, both gifted — yet in different realms.

As their older sister, I never considered myself extraordinary, but later I realized that the apple doesn't fall far from the tree. I was always complimented for being techie (as a woman), and for being creative. But it took many years to claim my gift of creativity and to recognize how my intuitive superpowers contributed to that. As a young adult, I would joke that I was psychic. It was just a joke because at that time I did not know any psychics. Later on, as a designer working with clients, I could "see" their entire brand before they even told me what they wanted. I've come to realize that I am telepathic and a channel. I receive many "downloads" and I channel guidance for my clients. Ideas and insights pour out of me, and I have an inner knowing of many things. I do not call myself a channel or an intuitive, but these gifts are what make me so insightful.

Are these gifts a passion? It's hard to say. It's just who I am. I believe my purpose is to be a conduit for ideas and divine inspiration. I have an uncanny ability to see the gap of what's missing and to create step-by-step processes to get things done (such as writing this book and developing the STAGES process).

It's difficult to articulate the invisible, and in many instances the English language doesn't include the words that describe what our gifts enable us to do. People tell me that I'm creative, so that's what I claim as my gift, although I know my superpowers go far beyond what words can describe.

Chapter 6

STAGE 5: Experience
What have you earned and learned over the course of your life?

"I am not what happened to me,
I am what I choose to become."

~ **Carl Gustav Jung** ~

experience — *the process of observing, encountering, undergoing or achieving.*

While *standards* are the moral code to living the life we long for, and *talents* and *gifts* are the innately expressive side of who we are, and *abilities* enable us to function in life, *experience* is what we've earned through certifications, degrees, and application, and it's also what we've learned through major events that we've been through, whether by choice or by chance.

Let me explain. We *choose* to pursue a career path and education, and those shape who we are and who we become. Then, events happen throughout life that disrupt our best-laid plans. Some are initiated by us, and others happen *for* us. Another way to put it is: Sometimes we choose our path, and other times our path chooses us.

We are attracted to certain people, places and things for a reason, but do you ever wonder why? Certainly, fate has played a part in the events of your past, and it will lead you to where you need to be in the future. I believe that this is your soul's destiny. If you trace the path of your past, you might notice a theme, a pattern, and a sudden twist and turn of events that led you to where you are now.

Some of these events may have been your choice, and others may have been coincidental, but I believe there's a higher power at play and we're all led to where we need to go to learn the lessons that prepare us to live into our fullest expression. We won't become self-actualized without actually experiencing our sense of self in all of its many dimensions.

We came here in this lifetime for a reason. Each and every one of us plays an important role, yet we tend to think of our lives as insignificant. You are anything but insignificant. You are a once-in-a-lifetime masterpiece. Your set of values, talents, abilities and gifts are unique to you and only you.

You are a piece of the puzzle we call *humanity*. Without you, there would be a hole left in that puzzle. And without your life experiences you would not be who you are now.

Look Around You

Your reality is a reflection of who you are. The people in your life are a mirror of what you attract as well as what you need to heal. Your experiences are a reflection of what you are uniquely capable of handling, and each one shapes you and the direction of your life.

Your experience is more than your degrees, certifications, or the positions you held in your lifetime, although they all add up to equal the person you are now. What you choose for your next stage of life will attract more experiences that determine who you are yet to become.

The cycles of life — we are born, die, and are born again — are consistent in every realm…in nature, in life, in your career. The losses you experience may be tragic and unexpected, but in many instances, you'll see that they created space for something better.

This STAGE is your life's resume — the qualifications that shape your future decisions. This goes beyond your degrees, certifications, awards and achievements. They all count for something, but what counts more is the experience of living.

For this STAGE, you're going to go as far back as you can remember and track your experiences. List memories and moments, as well as your degrees, career experience, what you've done and are uniquely qualified to do.

Reflect on each stage of life. You may not remember as far back as your years as an infant or toddler, but do your best to list eventful moments. Perhaps a sibling was born or a relative passed on. Or maybe your parents moved and your life was in flux. List anything of significance that had an impact on your life: friendships, breakups, even movies that changed your way of viewing life. Anything that had an impact is an experience. Do your best here. You may have to go through it a few times as memories start revealing themselves.

Birth to 1 year _____

_____

_____

Age 1-5 _____

_____

_____

Age 6-10 _____

_____

_____

Age 11-15 _____

_____

_____

Age 16-20 _____

_____

_____

Age 21-25 _____

_____

_____

Age 26-30 _____

_____

_____

Age 31-35 _____

_____

_____

Age 36-40 _____

_____

_____

Age 41-45 _____

_____

_____

Age 46-50 _____

_____

_____

Age 51-60 _____

_____

_____

After Age 60 _____

_____

_____

When you look at your list, what themes or patterns do you notice?

_____

_____

_____

What significant events can you carry into your next "evolution"?

_____

_____

_____

Are there any synchronicities or unexpected opportunities that had a major impact?

_____

_____

_____

Any other insights?

_____

_____

_____

Finally, think about any grudges or resentments that you need to forgive or release before moving on to the next chapter of your life. What can you let go of and clear the slate? Keep this in mind as we move on to the sixth and final STAGE of the process, where your experiences come together in a way that has the potential to impact thousands of lives.

~ Mindset Shifts ~

- These are your **Evolutionary Experiences**. They go beyond your degrees or certifications. They're about applying what you've earned in real life, and gleaning lessons from your life's events.

- Your experiences start the day you were born, even before that, if you consider the conditions or *zeitgeist* of society during the time of your birth. My youngest brother was born a few weeks after John F. Kennedy was assassinated. Mom talks about how the "vibe" in the hospital was sullen, as opposed to being born in the mid '50's when there was no war and the feeling was general hopefulness for the state of our country. Even having a sibling born after you is an event that changes the trajectory of what your life might have been had you been raised an only child.

- Life lessons hold the most value in your growth and are often an initiation into a spiritual awakening. A spiritual awakening occurs to get us onto our path to purpose. Often, it will help to reveal our greatest gifts, skills and talents, as well as qualities such as resilience and fortitude. We are creatures of comfort and until something wakes us up and moves us forward, we will stay content doing what we do, never venturing outside the edges of our comfort zone. Tracking the breakdowns before your breakthrough will leave clues on what you are truly here to do.

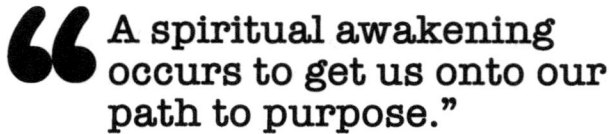

" A spiritual awakening occurs to get us onto our path to purpose."

~ My Story, Part 7 ~
My Life Path

When I was 6 months old my parents bought a home in Glassboro, New Jersey, a diverse college town. Growing up next to "the woods" with plenty of spaciousness was a much different environment than the blue collar town where we had an apartment. I loved living in a college town because many of my friends moved there from different states as a result of their parents getting teaching jobs. That's how I met my partner, Dr. Richard Grupenhoff, a transplant from Cincinnati, Ohio.

May 1999, at graduation for my M.A. in Public Relations at what is now Rowan University, with Richard, Mom, and Jason.

I joke that I'm a Diva because I was an only child for the first 2.5 years of life, before my brother Michael came along. I have vague memories of having to share Mom's attention with this beautiful new baby. I had to accept it because by the time I was 8 years old, I had 5 younger brothers.

At age 5, I expanded from the confines of our small town neighborhood and started Kindergarten in the same building that nearly 30 years later I would attend to earn two degrees, and soon after teach courses as an adjunct professor of Journalism.

I attended 1st through 4th grade at St. Bridget's Catholic School, basically in fear of doing something wrong and facing the wrath of the nuns. I saw plenty of classmates get whacked with a yardstick. They were not good memories and shaped my personality. I was shy and introverted.

In 5th grade I transferred to public school, where it was like one big out-of-control party. I learned quickly not to raise my hand

and show that I knew the answers. It was my first experience of having to dumb down. More suppression.

In middle school, awards were not handed out so freely, yet I was the only student in my grade to receive an award for most improved in Language Arts. Some of my fondest memories in high school are from English class and the books I read.

But, because I did not have much direction, and certainly did not feel ready for college, I got married at age 18, right out of high school, and at age 20 our son Jason was born. My husband and I would be divorced after 17 years of marriage.

It's not surprising that I reinvented my life at 50 because I was a late bloomer. When Jason was a toddler I had a longing to attend college, but it took another 10 years to register for my first course. The only class available to me was Economics. I sat there wide-eyed, absorbing new concepts that were foreign to me, yet I earned an A. Soon, my first writing professor, Dr. John Chard, would recognize my talent for writing and urge me to NOT continue to pursue a business degree. That changed the trajectory of my life. I ended up with a B.A. in Communications, and an M.A. in Public Relations because of the writing aspect.

My first job as an adult was the local library where, even though I did not have a degree, I became the default reference librarian. I was even offered a position as the director of another library, without having the required Master of Library Science.

If I were to compare my life to a movie, I'd be Chauncey the Gardener in *Being There*. Opportunities were presented to me over and over, without my having to pursue them. Things I thought I wanted didn't pan out and in retrospect I now see how they would have been a disaster. It's difficult to see it when you're in the middle of it, but life really does happen for you, not to you.

Chapter 7

STAGE 6: Story
What is the narrative of your journey to here?

"Once you start recognizing the truth of your story, finish the story. It happened but you're still here, you're still capable, powerful, you're not your circumstance. It happened and you made it through. You're still fully equipped with every single tool you need to fulfill your purpose."

~ Steve Maraboli ~

story — *the retelling of a narrative designed to inspire, interest, entertain, or instruct others.*

Your story has the potential to change – and even save – lives. It can be *that* powerful and could be the greatest contribution you make in the world if you choose to share it. *Story* brings us to the last stage of the STAGES Life Purpose Formula, and the most meaningful. While *standards, talents, abilities, gifts,* and *experiences* are a reflection of who you say you are, your story is where they all come together to reveal who you are for others. While your passion is about you, your purpose is about the impact you make on others.

Listing your experiences probably brought up a lot of ideas for stories that you could tell. Be judicious in your choosing. There's a time to tell each story. Blurt out your story to someone who is not interested or not ready to receive it, and it could fall on deaf ears.

Choosing the Right Story to Tell

Most of us have many stories that we could tell that others would find interesting. Because we have so many stories, starting from when and where we were born, who our parents are, where we went to school, and all the details in between, it's important to know what to include in the stories we tell and what to leave out, so they have greater impact.

I believe we all have what I call a *Soul's Calling Story* — how you came to do what you do — and that story holds a message within it that can impact others. Your soul's calling story isn't about you; its purpose is to relate to others in a way that they see themselves in it. It's where you piece together turning points in a cohesive string of events that come together in a meaningful and often emotional message.

Here are some different types of stories you could tell to different audiences at different times:

- ▶ If you're an entrepreneur, this could be your *origin story* — what led you to start a business or caused you to change direction.
- ▶ Your story might be of witnessing pain or suffering and wanting to change the world because of it.
- ▶ You could share the story of resiliency, how you got through a painful divorce, a health crisis, the loss of a loved one, or some other life-changing event to help others through a difficult time.
- ▶ You might have an inspiring story of how you lost 100 pounds, or an entertaining story of your escapades on the dating scene, or as a member of a rock band, or a rags to riches story, or a prophetic story of finding redemption in the church.

The ideas are endless, as long as your story has some level of value to the listener. The more emotional your story is, the better, because the purpose of story is to move people to act, to make them feel that they're not alone, and to inspire, entertain, and make them laugh.

Whatever story you choose to share, make sure it has a message and that you're speaking to the people who are receptive to hearing your message. There's no need to relate every detail, but you want to focus on the main turning points that got you from Point A to Point B. Turning points are related events that changed the trajectory or course of the time of life that your story is about. These can be actual physical events or they can be inner "ah-a" realizations.

The Breakdown Before the Breakthrough

I believe the Universe course corrects and puts us on a path to our destined purpose through breakdowns — big or small — that lead to breakthroughs. I've said before that life doesn't happen *to* us, it happens *for* us. We just need to be aware of the lessons that each turning point holds and how they fit into the bigger picture.

Often, it takes the passing of time to be able to share this type of story effectively because we have to heal before we can realize the life lessons that it holds for us. In my experience and observation, this takes about three years.

In STAGE 1, you came up with your personal big WHY. Often, your story is your bigger WHY; it's the impetus for you exploring and living your life purpose. You went through something remarkable — good or bad — and lived through it to share your lessons with others.

Make Your Mess Your Message, Make Your Message Your Movement

For this final STAGE, you'll use the outline on the following pages as a guide to write your story. "Make your mess your message, make your message your movement" is the premise of drawing on your life breakdowns to make change in the world by sharing the breakdown *and* the breakthrough. You may have several stories that were pivotal to putting you on the path you're on now. Not every story is going to be interesting enough to tell, so choose the one that has a message that will have the most impact on your audience.

You might choose to focus on stories around your work, around a cause, around the biggest events in life, around your passion… the important thing is to give meaning to each turning point and how it impacted you along the way. Every story has a beginning, middle, and end, so if you're writing about your "mess" you may not be able to write the ending of the story until you've integrated the lessons in a way that can be used to help others.

Write your Soul's Calling Story

You may not have reflected on the events of your life in this way before. We usually don't put two and two together to see how one thing led to the next, or why something happened the way it did until much later on. Your brain stays busy wondering why or how something could have happened, and it's much later on that you'll have an insight in an, "Oh, that's why that happened" moment.

When you reviewed your life path by listing your experiences, you may have recognized some patterns, or life lessons that were given to you. Take an experience that was a big "mess" in your life and create a message from it through a story. What lessons arose, and what can you use to teach or inspire others? Many entrepreneurs build a business around their story. Authors write entire books around their story. Your story really is the one thing you have that truly sets you apart from everyone else, because no one has the same story as you.

Do your best here. Use the outline as a starting point. You might want to journal around your story first and see what emotions arise. Emotions add power to any story, so be sure to include how you felt at the time and impart that emotion to your listener or reader.

Keep your story focused to a specific time frame and outcome. Unlike in STAGE 5, where you listed the major experiences in each phase of life, your main story is usually based on only one or two of the phases, although earlier phases may add background or details to your story.

You may want to draft several different stories and see which ones have the most potential to help others in some way, even if it's just to entertain.

What Events Got You to Where You are Now?

Before you approach the outline, use the following prompts to jog your memory — and your emotions.

From STAGE 5, choose the most impactful events that shaped your life as it is now.

_____
_____
_____
_____
_____

When you look at your life experiences is there a "before and after?" Where you started — Point A — to where you ended up — Point B.

_____
_____
_____
_____
_____

Was there anything you saw that was wrong that you took action to make right and it became your "cause" or your "stand?"

_____
_____
_____
_____
_____

These are all fodder for your Soul's Calling Story. When you write your story, make sure it has a beginning, a middle, and an end.

If you base your story on the premise that "Your mess is your message, your message is your movement" here are some guidelines:

> Your **mess** is the focus of your story, but you never want to present it as being a victim. Handling the mess takes courage. If you ran from it, you may never have embarked on the journey to overcome the challenges required to become who you are now.

> Your **message** is the moral of the story — the lesson, inspiration, advice that you want others to experience when you tell your story. Think *Aesop's Fables*. There was always a lesson.

> Your **movement** is the change that you can initiate through sharing your story. As with core values, this defines what you stand for in a bigger way — a movement has the power to change the world!

It's Your Turn to Write

Follow the outline as best as you can. Go deep and don't hold back. Add details that make it entertaining, inspiring, and emotional. Imagine that you're writing the screenplay of your life, with you in the starring role and each turning point a new scene.

What is your Point A – where you started; the beginning of your story. This sets the stage to show the calm before the storm.

_____
_____
_____
_____
_____
_____

Turning Point 1: This is typically an event that set change in motion or that upset your peace in Point A.

_____
_____
_____
_____
_____
_____

Turning Point 2: The mess, aka the ramification of Turning Point 1, and often the highlight of the story.

_____
_____
_____
_____
_____
_____

Turning Point 3: Another event, realization, observation, or ah-a that either made the situation worse, or started to turn things around. It's where you decided you would take matters in your own hands.

_____
_____
_____
_____
_____

What you did to make it right: The comeback, the fix, how you discovered a solution, or how you got help.

_____
_____
_____
_____
_____

Your Point B: How it turned out (your movement to share):

_____
_____
_____
_____
_____

The moral of your story: The message you want to share with the world to teach, heal, inspire, or motivate. Make this short and sweet in one or two sentences in the style of an *Aesop's Fable*.

_____

_____

_____

_____

_____

_____

Going through the story-writing process will reveal some deep-rooted beliefs and emotions. It might bring up even more memories than you listed in STAGE 5.

It's important that your story is empowering to you and to others. You never want to come away as the victim, and if your story is still painful make sure you can keep it together emotionally as you share it. This often takes a period of healing so you are on the other side and can look at the events through clear eyes and a clear mind.

You want to inspire others so you want to be the heroine of your story, who comes away victorious. When you do this, others will see themselves in your story, and also relate to coming away victorious if they're going through, or have gone through, similar experiences.

If you have a business, or are planning on starting a business, your story could be the WHY behind starting your business. You'll share your story on your website, on interviews, and you may even choose to write a book based on it.

This is the final, and most powerful, stage in the STAGES Life Purpose Formula. And it's the one that can have the most influence on others. When you impact lives through your story you are living your purpose.

~ Mindset Shifts ~

➤ Sharing your **Soul's Calling Story** can be your way of living your purpose and impacting lives. Even though it's your story, it can help others because they'll see themselves in your story.

➤ "Make your mess your message, make your message your movement" is a structure that many can relate to because everyone has had their own messy moments. Hearing yours provides solace and comfort to know that they are not alone.

➤ Your story is the one thing that sets you apart from everyone else. The key is to tell it in a way that is interesting and has meaning that others can relate to, whether it's entertaining, motivating, or emotional. It doesn't have to be profound but the way you tell it should elicit some sort of reaction. Think about Jerry Seinfeld. He tells stories about nothing. Millions of people are still laughing at them through reruns that they've watched umpteen times because we all relate to the mundane. It's his delivery that makes them hilarious!

NOTE: In the following excerpt of my story, I retell parts of what I already shared in a way where I plot out the turning points, so you can see how it all comes together. I call it my "inspiration story" because it illustrates the WHY of my becoming an entrepreneur and how I overcame limiting circumstances to create my own success. It leads to the moral of my story, which is: "We all have inherent VALUE. If I can become a successful entrepreneur, so can you, and I can show you how." This is the story that I used to tell to audiences of women who were emerging entrepreneurs.

~ My Story, Part 8 ~
My Mess, My Message, My Movement

Point A. Where I started out: At age 50 I walked out of my job of 18 years. Feeling burned out, I decided to give myself 6 months to figure out what I'd do with my life. I had no idea what I'd do, but I had no desire to start my own business.

Turning Point 1: I put together my resume and went on interviews. The callbacks I got were from nonprofits. I was surprised that corporate had no interest in my skills or experience, even though I held a master's degree in public relations and was assistant director of a leading global educational organization..

Turning Point 2 (The Mess): On EVERY job interview I went on, I heard some version of, "You're overqualified." Code for "We can't pay you enough." One women even said, "You wouldn't be happy here." The deal breaker was that none of the positions offered a vacation package that was close to what I was used to, which did not sit well with this Goddess, whose highest core value is *freedom*.

Turning point 3 (realization): Frustrated at the level of salary that those places were willing to pay to someone with my level of experience, I decided to create my own opportunities. I sat at my desk, head in my hands, and said to myself, "Okay, Carol Ann. You're going to try this entrepreneurship thing, but if you don't replace your salary from your J.O.B. you're going to have to go out there and find another one."

This is what I did: Almost exactly 6 months from the day I left my J.O.B. I marched down to the County office and registered my company, *Big Eye Media Design & Photography*. I calculated what to charge in alignment with my experience and expertise — above the going rate in my area. I joined a few networking groups, announced to my colleagues that I was open for business, and I was on my way.

Significant Ah-a: What I discovered is that my talents, gifts, skills, and experience were in high demand by small business owners who needed a creative to do the work they weren't capable of doing. They were willing to pay me top dollar because I delivered quality, and they were saving money because they did not have to hire a full-time employee. I had found my people — the ones who saw the value in my talent.

Point B: Even though I called myself a graphic designer and photographer, I became known as the "concept to completion" gal for everything marketing and publishing. I was an anomaly and that was a good thing. I would attend networking events and it was like people were throwing money at me! Those same gifts that I was turned away for were highly valued by the right people.

How it panned out: I made more than 6 figures my very first year because I knew how to monetize my skills and talents, and I stood in my value by charging more than the average rate because I provided good customer service and quality work. I survived the economic downturn of 2008, even when my peers were closing their doors. I continued to thrive because I did not go into a lack mindset or get caught up in the worry stories that were so prevalent at the time. That was a life lesson that showed me how success really is 80 percent mindset, and 20 percent strategy.

My Message: Everything you need is already inside of you. If you don't value yourself no one else will. Your gifts are needed in the world and it's your responsibility to do the inner work to get over your own limiting beliefs. Your people need you, and you've got to get out there so they can find you! *That* is the secret to success!

My Movement: "Sizzle to Success" became my movement, named for my first online program, *The Sizzle System of Personal Branding*. I developed a talk to empower women to recognize and OWN their VALUE, charge their worth and recognize the breakthrough in every breakdown.

The Moral of my Story: I am no different than you. If I can do it, so can you! Don't let others be the judge of your brilliance — stand in your value and get out there and SHINE!

In November 2015, I took my show on the road with a 4-hour workshop titled, Sizzle to Success. I shared my story, along with success tips to brand a business "from the inside out," along with many of the concepts I share in this book, starting with a core values assessment, which I also taught in my program, The Sizzle System of Personal Branding. Here I am with my Sizzlers at a workshop in Cherry Hill, New Jersey, leading them in my trademark move to show how 'Sizzlin' HOT" we are! It was a lot of fun, and several of the attendees went on to be long-term clients.

> "We might be through with the past, but the past ain't through with us."
>
> from the film, *Magnolia*

Ignite Your Passion • Find Your Purpose

PART II

The Next STAGE: Live Your Purpose

CHAPTER 8

Putting It All Together
Did you find your purpose?

"The two most important days in life are the day you were born and the day you find out why."

~ Mark Twain ~

purpose — *the reason for which something exists; an aim, intention, goal or desired result.*

Congratulations — you finished! How did you do? Did you identify your purpose? Are you at least closer to finding it? You might still feel as if you have some loose ends that need tying up, and that's what you'll do in this chapter.

STAGES is a soul excavation. It's designed to make you think. It's not like the Kolbe or Myers-Briggs, or any other personality test. This is a Life Purpose Reveal process. I hope you discovered some things about yourself. Perhaps memories revealed themselves — ones that you had long forgotten. If nothing else, I hope you have a different perspective on the events and turning points of your life.

This is a reminder of your brilliance, your specialness, and your deservingness. You, as much as anyone else, deserve to be happy, and to live a life of purpose doing what you love.

Now, I don't want to dismiss the fact that your life may not have been peaches and cream. I speak to many women who have had horrible experiences throughout their lifetime. If your brain dump turned into a "trauma dump" you may have to do the work to heal.

I suggest if some deep stuff came up for you, you seek professional help. It's when you heal that you can share your story as if you are separate from it, an observer, and see the blessing in it. Or, you may never see the blessing in it. Perhaps you are part of someone else's healing.

Awareness Is the First Step

STAGES is designed to bring you back to you despite all that you've gone through. It's when you turn your breakdowns around that you see the value and how resilient and amazing you are because, like most other women, you lived through some heavy crap.

If you're at a crossroad now, know that you will live through this, too. Once you learn how to accept the breakdowns and see that they are steps to a more courageous you, you become unstoppable. There's not a whole lot that you can't do.

Love & Gratitude

Before we move on, let's do some clearing. First, I want you to show yourself gratitude for going through this process. Next, show yourself gratitude for all you've been through over your lifetime. It was through all the past stages of life that got you here and made you the person you are today. Let's leave the memories behind and take the lessons as you move forward, along with all your amazingness and courage. Now, go look in the closest mirror, and tell yourself, "I love you." Notice your beauty, your strength, your passion. From this moment forward align with that person, your higher self, the woman who is capable of doing amazing things.

Clarity Is a Beautiful Thing

Going through your life stages is about what was. I get that you might still be wondering. What do I do with all this? What can I take away from each STAGE? Let's make it tangible and create a "nutshell" version of your results by gleaning the most important findings. For each question below, write a brief response. I use business as an example, but replace that with whatever endeavor feels right to you.

STAGE 1, Standards. This is what's most important to you overall. If you were to create a business, for example, what would you be working for? *Money freedom, recognition?* How would it support your life, and what is your bigger vision? *Leadership, influence, meaning...*

_____

_____

STAGE 2, Talent. What talents could you build a business around? Could you become a writer, an actor, a fashion designer, an artist?

_____

_____

STAGE 3, Abilities. What skills could you incorporate into your business? Not just at the core of the business but that would support you to be successful? *Marketing, finance, sales...*

_____

_____

STAGE 4, Gifts. What "superpowers" could add to your business delivery or be the delivery itself? *Hands-on healing, readings, reiki, intuition, creativity, insightfulness...*

_____

_____

STAGE 5, Experience. What experiences could you base your business on? *Life lessons, certifications, degrees, past jobs...*

_____

_____

STAGE 6, Story. What is your Soul's Calling Story about? The one you could use to share your message or start a movement...

_____

_____

Do you see how your passions are one thing, but your purpose is another? I bet your next question is: *Okay, so now that I'm closer to finding my purpose how do I start living it?* Keep reading because that's where we're headed next.

~ Mindset Shifts ~

- ➤ STAGES is not a personality test, it's a soul excavation to provide a bird's eye view of the events and experiences of your life so you see the value in each and how it has contributed to who you are now.

- ➤ If you are at a crossroad, know that whatever is going on won't last forever. You've showed great resilience in the past and you are capable of amazing things. Show gratitude to yourself for getting you through whatever mess was part of your life. Those are the events we tend to hold onto, and perhaps now is the time to let them go.

- ➤ Letting go of the past isn't always easy, but it's important to heal from any past trauma that may have been keeping you from moving forward. Seek professional help if necessary.

~ My Story, Part 9 ~
My Dark Night of the Soul

I took my business online in 2014 with the launch of my program, *The Sizzle System of Personal Branding*, to make money with what I know, not what I do. It was great and I was excited at the prospect of teaching women around the globe to create a "red hot" brand. But they still expected me to design logos and websites, and I had grown out of alignment with the work I had been doing for so many years. I was at a low point and, once again, felt that there was more for me. I had to change my identity. There was also a lot of craziness happening all around me that put me in a Dark Night of the Soul. Without rehashing the sordid details, I saw the evil side of some people. It is true that "haters gonna hate," and even though their behavior is more a reflection of who they are, it's not easy to take. I had a constant gnawing in the pit of my stomach that kept me frozen in fear, wondering what to do next. Then, October 20, 2015, Dad transitioned after a long journey with Alzheimer's Disease. That was the turning point that had me see that I had to step up and align with my higher purpose. Somehow I found the strength to empower myself to say, "OK, Carol Ann, you've had enough. This craziness has to end NOW, and you're going to move forward." And that's what I did. I reset to zero. I assessed my life path and searched for my purpose. That's when I developed the STAGES Assessment.

And then, out of the blue, women started reaching out to me, not for branding, but to help them find *their* purpose. It was uncanny, as if the Universe led them to me. It's not like I held up a sign that said, "I'm searching for my purpose. Can I help you find yours?" I was in no state of mind to help anyone!

But I did. And I healed my situation. I worked with a spiritual advisor, I meditated and prayed, and I "downloaded" an entire new brand, *AlignBelieveCreate on-purpose coaching*, being intentional about including the word *coaching*. My tagline included my values: "Align with Your Passion, Believe in Your Power, Create on Purpose."

Shortly after, in a healing session, the Goddess showed up. My "sub-brand" became The Goddess Way. I launched a new program, *Goddess Unleashed*. I started offering *Find Your Life Purpose Intuitive Readings*. This opened up the Divine Feminine side of my business that was so different from the logistics of branding. I had evolved into my higher purpose. I started taking clients through the STAGES Assessment. It was then that I started to coach clients on creating offers, messaging, speaking. I formed *The Goddess Way Inner Circle*, a sacred space for spiritual entrepreneurs. I loved bringing soul-centered women together.

But, helping women find their purpose opened my eyes to some things. It was quite disconcerting and confirmed what I once heard Jack Canfield say (paraphrased): "Deep down everyone knows their purpose, but few are brave enough to live it."

By now I was 60 years old and finally brave enough to live mine.

When we lost Dad I gained renewed strength and fortitude. I knew he would not want to see me in pain, or in fear. That was not his spirit or his way of being. I picked myself up and decided to do things my way – again. Here we are with Mom and my eldest brother Michael, circa 1958, when it was just the four of us. Before long it would be eight.

CHAPTER 9

Your Next Steps
How to Move Forward on Purpose

"Definiteness of purpose is the starting point
of all achievement."

~ **Mark Twain** ~

success — *the favorable or prosperous accomplishment of
one's goals or endeavors.*

Now that you see that passion is about what makes you happy, but purpose is how you contribute to something greater than yourself, how will you move forward to express your purpose in the world?

It depends on what you want to do. STAGES provides insight on what your soul is designed to do, and what you have to offer others, but you will still need the "vehicle" to be able to do it.

If you're like most women standing at a crossroad searching for meaning you would likely choose one of these paths:

➤ Volunteering and giving your talents away

➤ Got to Indeed and search for a J.O.B.

➤ Start a business

My stance is to put you first, do what you love to make the money you need to make, and when you're living in the overflow, give back in some way.

Getting another J.O.B. might seem like the easy route, but you might be replacing one crappy situation with another.

I work with entrepreneurs so I'm going to give you advice on how to start a business. Even if you have a business now, but you're not happy and want to pivot, you might want to do what I did and "reset to zero" so you're more aligned with your purpose. My core values for business are *simplicity* and *alignment*, so I'm always going to suggest the path of least resistance — based on your wisdom from your learned experiences, not sweat equity from your earned experiences.

What I suggest is based on nearly 20 years of experience combined with what's working at the time of writing this book. The online space has evolved quite a bit since the Great Resignation caused by the Covid Pandemic, so what worked in 2014 isn't necessarily working now, although some principles remain the same.

The number one mindset I want you to take away is this: a business exists to create an income. There are many other reasons to start a business, purpose being a close second, and freedom being a close third. But, first and foremost, you want to make sure whatever you start a business around is going to generate an income that you can live on. Be sure to charge appropriately for your gifts, talents and experiences, or people will not value them. Your passion will soon turn to resentment and you'll be looking for a J.O.B. just to survive.

Now that we've gotten that out of the way, the good news is that the barrier of entry is almost non-existent anymore when it comes to starting a business, especially an online business. I specialize with working with women over 50 to share their wisdom with the world so I'll stay in my lane and speak to what I see as the most likely path to success. The possibilities are endless to start a business based on your purpose, but the steps are different depending what your goals are.

I'm going to share first steps to take that will prepare you and help figure out what you are most cut out to do, and then I'm going to give you my top three ways that will get you farthest fastest. Know that this is a starting point and that you'll be learning as you go.

First Steps to Success

This advice is for you whether you're starting anew or you're switching your niche. "Switching your niche" simply means you are doing what you have always done, more or less, but in a different methodology or with a different audience. For example, if you spent your career as a nurse, and now you offer wellness services in a different capacity to private clients, you are taking your life's work and applying it in a different way. Success comes quicker when you stay in your lane rather than try to take on something you have no experience in.

Here are my Top 10 First Steps to Success:

1. Decide what you want to DO and who you want to do it FOR. Do you want to help women lose weight, heal their trauma, or perhaps you want to work with children. Again, stay in your lane.

2. You will need and offer to sell. This can be a service or a product. It takes a while to figure out how to get people to buy, and what they want. But you have to start somewhere.

3. Do your research to find out what others are doing in the area you choose. Don't be discouraged by competition. The more competition, the better. This shows there's a demand for it.

4. You will need an audience to sell to. Define who these people are, and then get in front of them somehow. Talk to people you know. Pay attention to their feedback, but take it with a grain of salt. Everyone wants to give their two cents, and often it's worth about that amount!

5. When you have a solid offer, attend free networking events. Most will allow you to attend one or two meetings before you'll have to join, so make sure you are ready to do business, and the group is made up of people who are likely to need your offer.

6. Call me old fashioned, but I believe every entrepreneur needs a business card. You can go on Canva and use a template for free and have a few printed up. Don't worry about getting it perfect. All you really need to start is your contact info. A business card is something you can leave with people as a reminder of how you can help them.

7. Access free resources on the internet to get a taste of what it takes to grow a business. Understand that you don't need to do all of what you see, and that free stuff only provides a piece of the larger puzzle.

8. Show up as a leader right away. Even if you're new at business, don't forget about the years of experience you have under your belt. If you spent 30 years in marketing for a retail store, and you decide to offer those skills to a different group of people, you are still an expert, so be sure to act like one — not a newbie!

9. Decide on your business model. Will you sell a product or service? Will you coach/consult/counsel clients in groups or individually? Will you hold events? This is bound to change and it's okay to make it up as you go along. That's how you'll gain clarity.

10. Hire a coach or mentor who can support you for where you are. This is an investment that will save you time and money in the long run. Until you have an offer that people want and an audience who will buy it — proceed cautiously in your investments.

This is a starting point. Don't try to do everything or you'll end up in overwhelm and won't do anything.

Top Three Ways to Share Your Purpose at Age 50+

You've got your first steps, but you will need a vehicle to deliver your purpose work. Here are my top three suggestions if you are over 50. Despite what you may have heard, there really is no fast path to cash, but you've got to start somewhere.

1. **Write a non-fiction book around your area of expertise.** This is going to position you as a thought leader right away, and you can sell your book on Amazon. Most likely, you will need a book coach, or an editor or ghostwriter to walk you through the writing and publishing process, but once you learn the ins and outs, you can publish a next book, then another, then another, and you'll increase your income while decreasing expenses.

   A book is your calling card. There are many ways to use a book to attract business, and to drive readers to your offer. Readers will need what you can help them with, and they'll want to follow up with you after reading your book. A book is a great way to drive people to a higher-end offer, or your book can be your offer.

2. **Become a speaker.** Join Toastmaster's and learn how to speak effectively. Develop a signature talk around the Soul's Calling Story you wrote in Chapter 7. Learn how to tell it with impact to move people to take action. Paid speaking gigs are hard to come by, but you can hold your own events and teach your area of expertise in a paid master class or workshop, either virtual or live. Once you have a signature talk, you can get featured on podcasts or in the media. You'll want to leave your listeners with a next step and a way to follow up with you, and that is how listeners become clients. A podcast gets you in front of other people's audiences, but you still need an offer. If you're just starting you can ask them to connect with you on social media. Or, if you have a book, you can offer that. Having a book will also lead to you getting invited to podcasts and other media interviews.

3. **Become a transformational coach/healer.** There are so many coaches nowadays that it's difficult to stand out unless you have a very specific area of expertise. In itself, being certified as a coach is not enough. It's the transformation you provide through your coaching that people pay for.

   For example, if you're a naturopath who helps women with fertility issues, or a weight-loss specialist, you can coach clients on your process. These are services that command top dollar when you lead with your expertise.

   No one buys coaching; they buy transformation! Same with healing. If you have a gift for healing then open a practice, but specialize and make sure you focus on the transformation, not so much on the modality. You can get certified in reiki, or massage, but what is the specific outcome that your sessions provide? That's what people pay for.

Other Ideas

There are a lot of get-rich-quick schemes around and a lot of noise on the internet. Here are some ideas you might be thinking of, so I want to offer a realistic view about them. They're not wrong, but they take more time and effort before you'll reap the benefits. And you've got to have some things in place first. It's better to create some success first, then embark on what I'm about to share.

Blogging. If you're not ready to write a book and you like to write, you might start a blog around your area of expertise. A cooking blog has huge potential. You still have to share it, do the SEO, and it takes a good 6 months for search engines to recognize it.

Courses. In my experience, many people who reach retirement age want to create a course. Fact is, unless you're known and you know how to market, you'll be spending a lot of time trying to sell your course, and you'll need an audience to sell to.

Affiliate marketing/direct marketing. This is not a way to live your purpose. You might hear that it's a way to make easy money but I know people who tried this and it took two years to make $10. You don't have that much time.

Yoga. You may have a vision of leading others in their sun salutations, but it doesn't pay. Even if you open a studio or teach on YouTube there's a lot of work to do upfront. To teach, you'll need your 200-hour certification. You might never make that money back, and you certainly won't get your time back! Really think about this one.

Done-for-you services. Copywriting, web design, or becoming a virtual assistant are skills that you can parlay into a business, but they're limited in the number of clients you can take on, and you still have to market to stand out from the crowd.

Final Thoughts

I'm here to help you live your purpose and if it's through a business I want you to stand in your value and get paid your worth. That's my mission, remember?

The one thing that I do know is that when you're doing your purpose work, you are more likely to be successful than if you started a business just for the money.

A business is the long road. If you're 50 you have a good 15 years to make your business work. If you're 60, I'd focus on something that does not require much building, but is more about sharing your wisdom and expertise as a leader, such as a book, or starting a podcasts of your own.

The important thing is to get started now. You will have missteps and false starts. That's normal and it's way better than waiting until you have it 100 percent figured out, because you will never have it figured out 100 percent! Business is a huge guessing game, and the fittest will survive, as you will see in the following chapter.

~ Mindset Shifts ~

- ➤ It's more important that you make a decision to START living your purpose than it is to wait until you have certainty on HOW to do it. You will have many missteps, false starts, and obstacles to overcome, but the sooner you get started, the sooner you'll get your purpose out into the world.

- ➤ Every business needs these two things: an offer that people want and an audience who will pay for it. It may take a while for you to get your offer right, which relies on communicating how you help, and it takes a while to build an audience. But, every successful business owner started at ground zero and built from there. At 50, you have decades of experience and expertise that people will pay for, so you're way ahead of the curve in many ways.

- ➤ There is no such thing as an overnight success or a fast path to cash as many will lead you to believe. The number one way to save time and money and to accelerate results is to hire a mentor who will support you to do what you need to do in the right order.

> **❝ I'm always going to suggest the path of least resistance, based on your wisdom from learned experiences, not sweat equity from your earned experiences."**

~ My Story, Part 10 ~
My Purpose Manifested

You may be wondering about my purpose and why I decided to write this book. I developed STAGES shortly after my "Year of Crazy" when I had fallen out of alignment with the work I had been doing for so long.

I went online in 2014 with my online program, *The Sizzle System of Personal Branding* when I realized personal branding was based on all I knew from earning an M.A, in Public Relations, PLUS I had the skills to create the visual elements that clients wanted.

I stayed in that lane because it made sense. But in going through the STAGES Life Purpose Formula, I realized that I was going back and forth between my Zone of Competence, Zone of Excellence, and even my Zone of Genius. These are terms coined by Gay Hendricks in his book, *The Big Leap*. After STAGES I took that one step further and coined the term, *Zone of Purpose*.

You may have a good guess at what I discovered my purpose to be. Even though I'm writing a book about helping you to find your purpose, that's not it. My purpose goes back to middle school when I won that award for most improved in Language Arts. I had no idea that would set the tone for what was to come.

My Purpose Started With a Vision

In 1987, my husband and I took our son Jason on a road trip from New Jersey to Disney World in Orlando, Florida. As we approached Orlando, we stopped at a red light. Something told me to look up — that whispering voice — and there was a skyscraper that stood above all the rest of the buildings, gleaning in the sunlight as if the sun's rays were shining a light on the letters on the side of the building for me to see. HBJ stood for Harcourt Brace Jovanich, a large publishing firm. I got a chill that caused me to pause and say to myself, "Someday, I am going to work in publishing." I never told this to anyone until now.

Who knew, that a year later, in 1988, I would be involved in publishing a book, and that would be the start of a long publishing career, with more opportunities falling into my lap.

What started my love of books and the written word started years earlier. When Jason was around 2 years old, Mom gave me a copy of *The Thorn Birds*. It sparked my interest in reading books and I started to take Jason to the local library every week, where I would bring home stacks of books for him and for me.

A few years later I would end up working at that library, becoming the default reference librarian when the woman with the MLS suffered from an injury and couldn't do her job effectively.

That led to me being offered a job as director of a new library in our county, without having a degree! I was so excited at the prospect of being the decision maker to purchase and be around so many books. That would not be my fate, though.

One day, as I was in between ending the job at the local library to start working at the new library, I was walking to the nearby post office. My friend Elouise, who also worked at the library for awhile, came running out of the building next store. She was waving a book and practically begged me to apply for a secretarial position at the educational organization she was now working for. The founder needed help. I was an emphatic "No." Why would I want to be a secretary when I could be director of a library? She persisted; I resisted. Finally, when they raised the starting salary to much higher than what the library paid, I accepted.

Even though Elouise had given me a book published by this company, I had no idea I would be so immersed in publishing books, curriculum projects, newsletters, and even videos, just one year after having that vision of HBJ.

In 1990 another friend I had reunited with when she came to work at the library suddenly moved to Las Vegas and handed down to me the arts newsletter that she was editing at the time. I took it a step further because I had the skills and I would interview artists, photograph them, then write articles, design the pages and had it published. Dad used to call me Murphy Brown. I did it all. I became the editor of several other newsletters, winning several awards.

On top of it, I was offered teaching positions at the university in the Art and Journalism departments. I taught Publications Layout & Design for 10 years!

Then, as an entrepreneur one member of our networking group was starting a magazine. She wanted me to be the editor. I ended up publishing three of them for many years. I was also asked to be part of the publishing team for an Italian newspaper.

Fast forward to 2016, two years into *The Sizzle System*, when a business colleague reached out to me to be part of her book giveaway event. Her assistant said, "Carol Ann, you must have a book, don't you?" I lied and said. "Yes, of course." I had tried to write a book but hated the process I was following, so obviously it was not the book I was meant to write.

Instead, I wrote a branding book based on *The Sizzle System* in less than 4 weeks. Who knew that *Girlfriend, we need to talk about your brand...* would have such a significant impact on my life. I had the most downloads of anyone in that giveaway event, and I also sold it for $17 online. Ultimately I created a course around it called the *Brand-athon* and attracted 40 clients who paid me between $47 and $197. It did not make me rich, but it got me through my transition period as I was shifting back into alignment with my purpose work.

That's not the end of the story, though. In 2017 I had an opportunity to attend a book writing conference in Princeton, where the investment to join their write a book in a weekend program was $40,000. It was not my style, but I took away what I learned.

I wrote an online article about my experience posing the question, "Is it possible to write a book in a weekend?" A client responded and said he wanted information. I knew this person would not want to invest $40,000, so I took what I knew about book writing and created a 90-day process that took 20 minutes a day.

He did not move forward so I put it aside until....

Months later, I ran a 3-week course, *Get Real. Get Raw. Get Writing* based on "make your mess your message, make your message your movement." I made an offer for clients to continue working with me and one said, "Carol Ann, do you know what I really want you to help me with? I want to write a book."

I almost fell out of my chair. She had no idea but I said, "It just so happens that I created a process to help you do that."

I easily filled my first group cohort of *Just Do It Write Now, Start Your Movement 90-day Book Plan*. Clients loved it! More important, they became published authors of books they were proud of!

I created that process in blind faith, and it just pured out of me. Somehow I knew there would be a purpose for it, because it was based on my purpose! STAGES showed me that books, publishing, and writing are what I'm here to do.

There's more to this story and how I found the courage and confidence to lead others to become published authors, but I want to bring you back to how it started — with a vision that came out of the blue, that would manifest into reality with a series of events that seemed to just fall into my lap. I never worried about HOW I would make any of it happen, and at the time had no desire to make it happen, but somehow the pieces fell into place and here I am living that vision, not working for a publishing company but BEING that publishing company!

Two of the first clients to go through my Just Do It Write Now process in 2018-19. I am so proud of them and honored that they chose me as their book mentor.

With Sherita Sparrow and her first book, Boss Artist. *Sherita is the reason I ran the program when she asked me to help her write her book. I also helped her write her second book,* The Healing Artist, *when I ran the program again in 2020.*

Here I am with Brenda Hornung at the 2019 Collingswood Book Fair. Brenda had been trying to write her book for 10 years before our paths crossed. Now, she is the proud author of Love Life Again, *to help woman who are going through a mid-life crisis.*

CHAPTER 10

Mindset 101 ~ Resistance, the Invisible Force

"If you can tune into your purpose and really align with it, setting goals so that your vision is an expression of that purpose, then life flows much more easily."

~ Jack Canfield ~

resistance — *opposition offered by our mind to block our success in an effort to keep us safe.*

I hope you're excited at the prospects ahead of you. If you're at a crossroad and trying to figure out what to do with the rest of your life, hopefully, you've put your past behind you and are ready for a fresh start.

Imagine standing at your crossroad, and instead of feeling alone and confused, you perceive the crossroad to be an opportunity to move forward in life-altering transformation. Reframing your thinking about a situation can turn negative thoughts to positive ones. I'm not saying it's as easy as putting lipstick on a pig and calling it pretty, but shifting the negative to positive can be a beacon of light to lead you to living your best life.

We are always at choice. It's no secret that many nurses and hospice workers relate stories of watching patients on their deathbed share their most common regret, and those regrets almost always include a dream they did not pursue. When you look back at your life's experiences, you may not have had the maturity to understand that you really are in control of your future. At age 50, your best years really are ahead of you.

It's not that easy to flip a switch on thoughts and behaviors that rise up as a result of emotional triggers. They affect us at the subconscious level that we're not even aware of. But with maturity, you gain the wisdom and wherewithal to weather just about any storm.

The Invisible Force that Keeps Us Stuck

It really is true that success is 80 percent inspiration, 20 percent strategy. In the last chapter I gave you some strategies. They're super important. But it doesn't take long for any business owner to realize that entrepreneurship is as much a journey of personal development as it is business savvy.

You will constantly be required to push against the edges of your comfort zone, and you will find every excuse to instead go eat that pizza that's in the fridge rather than email a contact or pick up the phone. You won't even be aware of your self-sabotaging behavior.

In his book, *The War of Art*, Steven Pressfield says that most of us have two lives: the life we live and the unlived life within us. Between the two stands Resistance, the most destructive force on the planet. He says that resistance stunts us and makes us less than we are born to be. He also says that if you believe in God, you must declare Resistance evil, for it prevents us from achieving the life God intended for us when He endowed each of us with our own unique genius. I wrote before that I believe we were given gifts from God, the Universe, Source or whatever higher force you believe in, to be able to support ourselves in the lifestyle we deserve. It's our responsibility to get our gifts out into the world, but that invisible force will continue to tell us that it's not safe to do so.

We're not even aware when Resistance shows up because it feels like our best friend. We've been living with procrastination and excuses all our lives. We're seldom aware of where they came from.

If you are at a crossroad, whether it's a voice calling you or a life event that is shattering your world as you know it, this really is your opportunity to have life your way. Embarking on something new and exciting may not be easy, but it doesn't have to be hard. If you understand that like anything there will be challenges along the way, you will find the power to rise and meet them.

Future Frequency v. Failure Frequency

Remember that when you set out to live your life purpose you are aligning with your higher self. You've got a vision of success. A vision is always in the future, so you're always moving toward it. If you keep your thoughts, behaviors, and actions aligned with that higher version of yourself your vision will manifest sooner rather than later. How do you do that? Faith. Stay in what I call your Future Frequency, positive expectation that you will have what you desire. If you're not used to having those desires they may seem too far out of reach. Don't let that discourage you.

Whatever vision you hold, when you hold it consistently and have faith that it is possible for you, it will become a reality. It might not happen tomorrow, or next year, but it will happen when you are ready for it. Get ready to be ready.

You have a much better chance of success when you align with your Future Frequency, rather than what I call Failure Frequency. In years of coaching clients, I see this all too often. Their program doesn't fill as they would like or an email doesn't get results, and they default to blame and shame. Of course, it's important to feel your feelings, but it's also important to pick yourself up and course correct, rather than feeling defeated. Half the time we're not even aware of resistance because it works at the subconscious. Our brain creates protective mechanisms that it thinks will keep us safe. Expect to experience failure. Some things won't work out. Much of what you're doing will be an experiment. There will be a learning curve. Every time you try to expand, that invisible force will push you back into the center of your bubble.

When something doesn't work out, know that it's perfectly normal. Try something else. Do what you can to shift your energy and your thoughts to match the frequency of your desires, not the failure. There is no failure, just experiments.

Try to avoid knee-jerk reactions. To be a leader of your life be conscious of your reactions as well as anxiety that shows up out of nowhere. Living on purpose is a practice and staying in neutrality will help you move through the tough times — you've already lived through some stuff, so take the courage you gained and remember how powerful you really are.

Remember that voice whispering to be more, have more, do more? There will be an opposing voice saying things like, "Who do you think you are?" "What makes you think you can have what you want?" "What makes you think you have what it takes?" You've got to ignore THAT voice EVERY time you hear it, and listen to the voice that is calling you to be more, do more and have more!

Trust me. If I can shift my life in a different direction after 18 years of going through the same motions, day after day, so can you. You've read my story and I want to remind you that I was a small town girl, with only a handful of people recognizing my brilliance and encouraging me to be more and do more.

I did not "find myself" until everything broke down and I was forced to examine my life. Experiencing what you don't want, always leads to something better. And that's the key to living your best life ever!

~ My Story, Part 11 ~
My Mindset Shift

It's not easy, going through a Dark Night of the Soul, and I wonder what life would have been like had I not. Similar to Groundhog Day, I imagine.

I don't know too many people who haven't had their share of dark times. It's part of life. I am a better person for it, and it opened me up to many experiences I wouldn't have had otherwise.

Dallas, Texas, at 50,000 feet, 2013.

It doesn't take long before you see how you'll always be led back to your purpose when you get off track. I didn't get back on track on my own. I found the right people. One of them was a mindset coach, Dan LeFave, a dude from Canada whom I happened to hear speaking online. He was exactly the type of coach I was looking for, and once again, I believe the stars aligned to put him in my path.

Working with him required a hefty investment, but after being in the 'void' for three years, I knew I had to take the risk. He helped me turn things around and within 30 days I enrolled a client who paid me the exact amount. He guided me to fill my book program with a one-question survey. All of a sudden life got easy. I "flipped the switch" and never went back to that dark place.

Sometimes you have to jump in with faith and courage. Or, you can jump from the sky at 50,000 feet. Both are risky, and equally exhilarating. Like Jack Canfield says, it takes courage to live your purpose. But when you do, you know you've done your best.

~ EPILOGUE ~
My Best Life, Here and NOW

As I approach age 70, it's hard to believe I've come this far. I've been in business for nearly 20 years. It's been a roller coaster with its ups and downs but it's the most thrilling ride I've ever been on. If I had to do it all over again I wouldn't change a thing (except maybe come back as Sophia Loren, or Oprah, or Patty Sciafa... but I digress).

As I entered 2024 I decided to change my identity from marketer to writer. After 10 years, I hung up my hat as a coach to do my purpose work: writing books and helping other women and a few good men write theirs.

I've rebranded from AlignBelieveCreate on-purpose coaching to Goddess55 Publishing, in alignment with that vision I had back in 1987 and with what STAGES revealed for me in 2018.

It's my latest evolution, but it may not be my last. I've got a lot of living to do. I intend to live to 111 (my birthday is 1-11), happy, healthy and whole, but if it's not in the larger plan, then what will be will be. I'm grateful that I am living my best life now, and my wish is that you are living yours, too.

The secret to living my best life? Doing my purpose work, laughing often, and spending time with people I love. It's simple, really.

~ Acknowledgments ~

I'd like to express gratitude to some pretty amazing people...

First and foremost, to my partner, Dr. Richard Grupenhoff, for his love and his patience.

To my besties, Maryann, Ruthann, Kathy, Marie, and Diane, all Gifted Goddesses in their own right.

To Michelle Kulp for her invaluable insight to motivate me to finish this book.

To my mentors over the years, especially Dr. Venus Opal Reese, who taught me to heal my heart; Dan LeFave, who elevated my mindset and gave me confidence to turn things around; and Elizabeth Purvis, for her teachings of The Standards, frequency and leadership.

To my parents, Sam and Grace DeSimine, for all they've done to make me who I am, along with my five brothers, Michael, Steven, Christopher, Richard and Joseph, and my extended family.

To my son, Jason Newlin, for being his own person, no matter what, and his partner, Cindy Decker, for allowing him to.

And the lights of my life, Charly Grace and J.T. Newlin, who amaze me with their talents every single day.

And to Bruce Springsteen, for always assuring me that things are gonna be alright.

~ Additional Resources ~

- For more information and additional resources visit www.Goddess55.com
- To access a FREE audio training and workbook that the STAGES Life Purpose Formula is based on titled, *Monetize Your Brilliance*, go here: stages.Goddess55.com
- For a FREE interactive workbook, *5 Steps to Becoming a Published Author in Just 20 Minutes a day*, go here: 5steps.Goddess55.com
- Other books by Carol Ann DeSimine:

  Girlfriend, we need to talk about your brand... Go from Stuck to Sensational in 90 Days: Your Step-by-Step Brand Plan, available on www.Amazon.com

- Recommended reading:

  The Big Leap: Conquer Your Hidden Fear and Take Life to the Next Level by Gay Hendricks, published May 2010, available on www.Amazon.com

  The War of Art: Break Through the Blocks and Win Your Inner Creative Battles by Steven Pressfield, published 2002, available on www.Amazon.com.

To contact Carol Ann directly, email her at carolanndes12@gmail.com with PURPOSE in the subject line.

Additional photo credits: Richard Grupenhoff, Kate Messinger, Bill Hornung.

~ About the Author ~

Carol Ann DeSimine is a writer and former branding and business coach. She lives in Mantua, New Jersey, a suburb of Philadelphia, PA, with her partner Dr. Richard Grupenhoff, a writer and retired film professor.

Her passions are creative self-expression, being in nature, hanging out with her girlfriends and grandkids, watching standup comedians and Bruce Springsteen.

Her purpose is helping other women to get their Goddess Gifts out into the world and share their wisdom through writing and creative self-expression. And to have fun doing it. Because if it's not fun, you might as well sit on the beach and enjoy life that way. No pressure.

Ignite Your Passion, Find Your Purpose is her second book but it won't be her last.

> "What a long, strange trip it's been."
>
> ~ Jerry Garcia ~

www.ingramcontent.com/pod-product-compliance
Lightning Source LLC
Chambersburg PA
CBHW070306230526
45470CB00002B/745